How we USE materials

Plastic

Holly Wallace

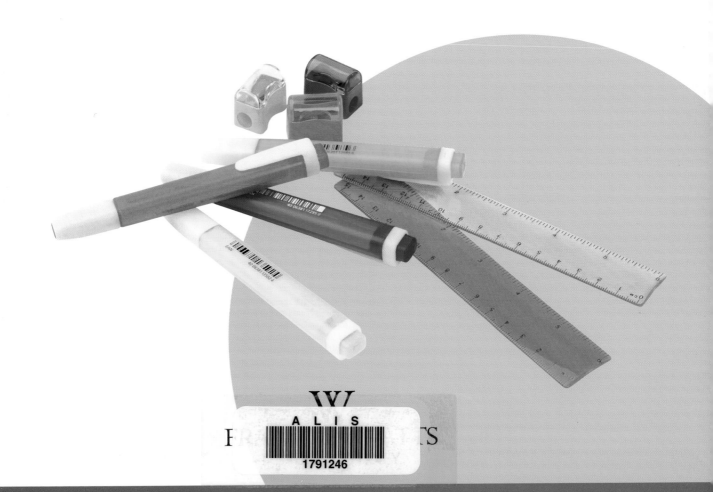

First published in 2006 by
Franklin Watts
338 Euston Road
London NW1 3BH

Franklin Watts Australia
Hachette Children's Books
Level 17/207 Kent Street
Sydney NSW 2000

Copyright © Franklin Watts 2006

Art director: Jonathan Hair
Series designed and created for Franklin Watts by Painted Fish Ltd.
Designer: Rita Storey
Editor: Fiona Corbridge

Picture credits:
Corbis p. 22 (left); General Mill Supply Co. p. 27; istockphoto.com p. 8, p. 20 (top),
p. 23 (top), p. 26; Tudor Photography pp. 6–9, pp. 10–20, p. 21 (bottom), p. 22
(right), p. 23 (bottom), p. 24, p. 25.

Cover images: Tudor Photography, Banbury

ISBN-10: 0 7496 6456 8
ISBN-13: 978 0 7496 6456 5
Dewey classification: 668.4

A CIP catalogue record for this book is available from the British Library.

Printed in China

Contents

Words in **bold** are in the glossary.

What is plastic?

Plastic is a **material**.
We use plastic to make
lots of different things.

Look around you. How many things
can you see that are made from plastic?

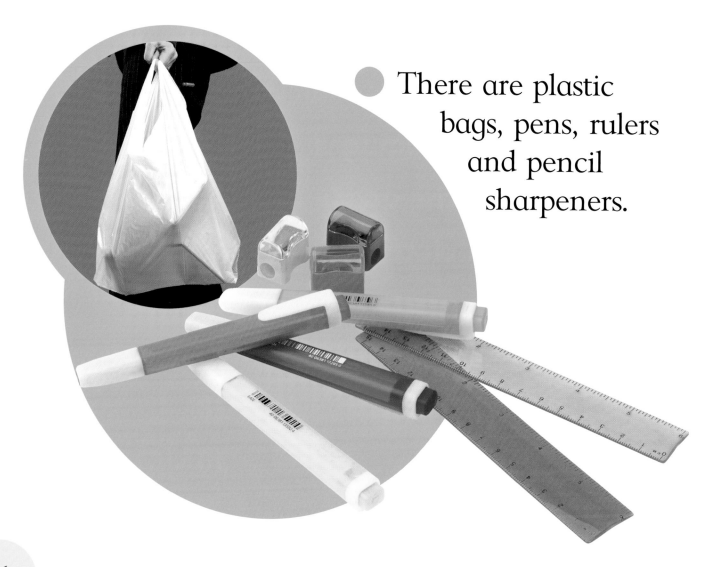

There are plastic
bags, pens, rulers
and pencil
sharpeners.

Plastic is a useful material because it is light, strong and **waterproof**. The cover and handle on this umbrella are plastic.

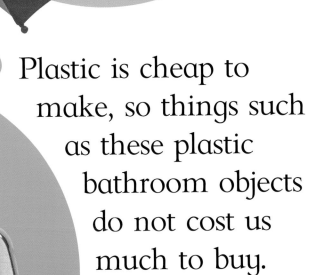

Plastic is cheap to make, so things such as these plastic bathroom objects do not cost us much to buy.

Plastic keywords

Material
Waterproof
Strong
Light

Where does plastic come from?

Plastic is not a **natural** material. It is made in factories from **chemicals**.

Most of the chemicals come from **oil**. The oil comes from under the sea or underground.

● We drill for oil from oil rigs.

In the factory, the chemicals are used to make tiny **chips** of plastic. The chips are now ready to be made into different plastic objects.

The chips are heated up so they melt and become a liquid. The liquid plastic is poured into **moulds** to make different shapes, such as these baskets. The plastic cools and goes hard.

Plastic keywords
Chemicals
Oil
Moulds

What is plastic like?

There are lots of different kinds of plastic. We use them for many different jobs.

● These boxes and this mobile phone are made of strong plastic. It does not break easily.

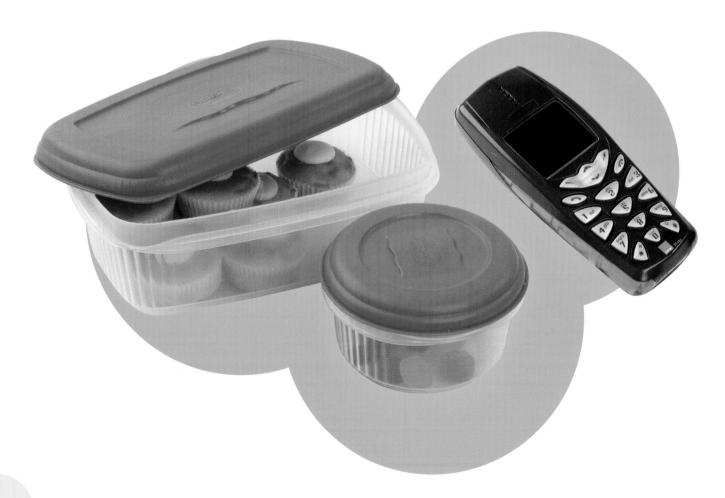

Some plastic is soft and easy to **bend**. These drinking straws are made from bendy plastic.

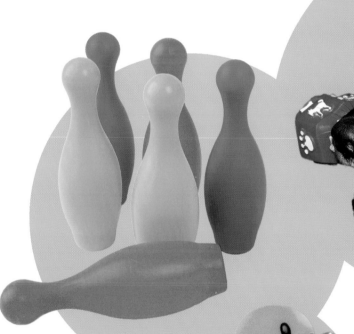

Plastic can be made in many colours. We use coloured plastic to make toys.

Plastic keywords
Soft
Bendy
Coloured

11

Plastic in buildings

Plastic is strong and waterproof. This makes it good for using in buildings.

Plastic pipes carry used water from baths and sinks.

Other pipes help rain to run away from buildings. Plastic is good for pipes because it lasts for a long time and is waterproof.

We sometimes make window frames from plastic instead of wood. This is because plastic does not **rot** like wood does. These frames are made from a plastic called **PVC**.

Pipes that go under the ground are often made from plastic instead of metal. This is because plastic does not go **rusty** like metal does.

Plastic keywords

PVC

Plastic in the home

Lots of the things in your home are made from plastic. How many can you find?

Some plastic is thick and strong. It is made like that so it will be **hard-wearing**.

Hard-wearing plastic is good for making things that we use a lot, such as vacuum cleaners and CD players.

Some plastic is **transparent**, this means we can see through it. Transparent plastic also lets light shine through it. It is useful for things like the end of this torch.

Plastic can be thin. This shower curtain is made from a thin, bendy sheet of plastic. It is waterproof.

Plastic keywords

Hard-wearing
Transparent
Thin

Plastic in the kitchen

Plastic is very useful in the kitchen. It is hard to break and safe to use for **containers** that hold food and drink.

This bowl is plastic. Plastic is waterproof and does not let liquids through it. Bendy plastics are good for making squeezy bottles.

Heat cannot flow through plastic well. So when we use plastic **utensils** to stir hot food, the handle does not get hot.

This plastic **vacuum flask** will keep liquids inside it hot.

Bins are often made of plastic because plastic is easy to clean.

Plastic keywords

Safe
Clean

Plastic packaging

Many different kinds of plastic are used to make **packaging.**

Plastic packaging holds and **protects** the things we buy in the shops.

Some packaging is transparent to show us what is inside. The plastic can also be **printed** with words and pictures.

We use thin sheets of soft, stretchy plastic for wrapping food. This keeps it fresh and clean.

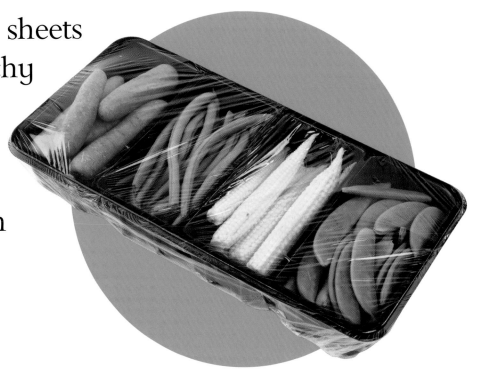

A light plastic called **polystyrene** is used to make takeaway food boxes. It helps to keep the food warm.

Plastic keywords

Packaging
Polystyrene
Stretchy

Plastic in the garden

Plastic is very good for making things that we use outdoors, too.

- Some garden tools are made from plastic because it is strong and does not go rusty.

Plastic is good for watering cans because it is waterproof and light.

Flowerpots can be made from clay or plastic. A plastic pot lasts longer than a clay pot and does not break so easily.

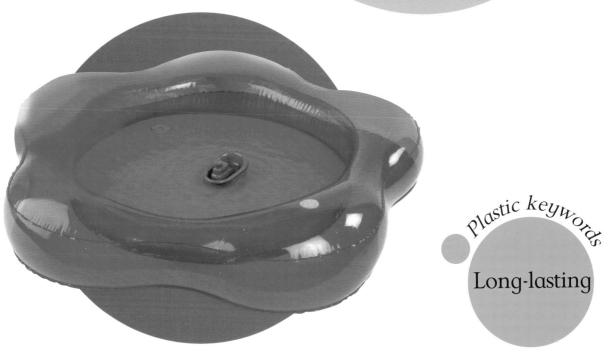

Plastic keywords

Long-lasting

This paddling pool is made from thin plastic. It is bendy so that you can blow it up. When the air is let out, the pool can be folded up and put away.

Plastic in clothes

Did you know that some of the clothes you wear are made from plastic?

- Plastic can be spun into long threads called **fibres**. Then the fibres are **woven** together to make pieces of fabric.

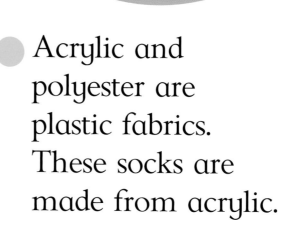

- Acrylic and polyester are plastic fabrics. These socks are made from acrylic.

This fleece top is made from polyester. The fabric is warm and does not **crease**. It does not go baggy.

We need plastic boots on rainy days. They are waterproof, so we can jump in puddles and our feet will not get wet.

Plastic keywords

Fibres
Woven
Fabric

Plastic in transport

Because it is light and strong, plastic is used to make parts of cars, bikes and planes.

● Plastic is easy to make into shapes, such as the different parts of this car dashboard.

Transparent plastic is used instead of glass for things such as lights on cars and bikes. Glass can hurt people if it gets broken, so it is safer to use plastic.

The wings and body of this small aeroplane are made from plastic. This helps to keep the plane very light so it will fly easily.

Recycling plastic

Plastic is a very useful material because it does not rot. But this causes problems.

When we throw plastic things away, they last for ever. This makes lots of rubbish.

Plastic bottles do not rot in the ground.

We can use some plastic again by melting it. Then it is made into chips. The chips are made into new plastic things. This is called **recycling**.

If we recycle plastic, it means that factories do not have to use up more of the Earth's oil to make new plastic.

This traffic cone is made from recycled plastic.

Plastic keywords
Rubbish
Recycling
Melting

Glossary

Bend Make into a curved shape.

Chemicals Special substances used to do many jobs, including making plastic.

Chips Small pieces.

Containers Boxes used for storing food and other things.

Crease Go wrinkly.

Fibres Long, thin pieces of a material.

Hard-wearing A material which is tough and strong, and lasts for a long time.

Material Something out of which other objects can be made.

Moulds Shapes that runny plastic is poured into to make plastic objects in those shapes.

Natural Comes from the Earth, plants or animals.

Oil Thick black liquid found underground or under the sea. It is used for fuel and to help make many other things.

Packaging The wrapping or containers used for storing the things we buy.

Polystyrene A type of light plastic.

Printed Marked with words or pictures.

Protects Stops things getting spoiled or harmed.

PVC A type of plastic called polyvinyl chloride.

Recycling Using a material again.

Rot To go soft and crumbly.

Rusty When some types of metal get wet, a browny-red substance called rust forms on them. Rust eats away the metal and makes it weaker.

Substance The material that a thing is made up of.

Transparent Clear or see-through.

Utensils Spoons, scoops and other tools used in the kitchen.

Vacuum flask A bottle that keeps liquids hot or cold.

Waterproof Does not let water pass through.

Woven Weaving fibres together (threading them in, out and around each other) to make a fabric or cloth.

Index